M000313330

WELCOME *to the* FAMILY *of* GOD

BEGINNING A NEW LIFE IN CHRIST

by Sandy Adams

NEW BELIEVER'S HANDBOOK

Welcome to The Family of God

By Sandy Adams

Published by The Word For Today

P.O. Box 8000,
Costa Mesa, CA 92628
(800) 272–WORD
Web site: http://www.twft.com

© 1979 The Word For Today
ISBN: 978-0-936728-22-3
2012 Printing

Printed in the United States of America

Welcome to the Family of God

A Reason to Rejoice

Congratulations, you've become part of God's eternal family. In Luke 15, Jesus tells the story of a woman who lost a coin. Being on a tight budget, she couldn't afford to throw away her money so she postponed her plans and searched for the coin until it was found. Once she had retrieved the coin she was so delighted she called her friends together to celebrate. What was lost had been found!

In verse 10, Jesus compares you to the coin. He said, "Likewise, I say to you, there is joy in the presence of the angels of God over one sinner who repents." God created you to live with Him, and without Him you were lost. God went out of His way to track you down. When you finally opened your life to Jesus, all God's angels erupted with joy. God really loves you! Your commitment to Christ has given heaven a reason to party! Welcome to the family of God!

Your decision to follow Jesus Christ is the most important decision you'll ever make. However, it might surprise you to discover that God chose you long before you chose Him. In Ephesians 1:4, God says that He had His eye on you before the foundation of the world.

From Rags to Riches

We all love "rags to riches" stories. Most of us are familiar with the saga of Rocky Balboa, a two-bit, punch-drunk, has-been boxer, who was chosen for a once-in-a-lifetime opportunity to fight for the heavyweight championship of the world. Rocky wins and instantly a nobody became a somebody. Your story is just as dramatic.

In a spiritual sense, God has lifted you from rags to riches. When you gave your life to Christ, God took you from death and darkness to life and light, from guilt to glory, from bondage to blessing, from a cell in hell to a mansion in heaven. You've become somebody special in Christ! Once a slave to sin, you're now a child of God. What a privilege it is to be a member of His family!

Try to imagine the richest man in the world adopting you as his son or daughter. Without lifting a finger, you automatically become the recipient of enormous privileges and blessings. When you gave your life to Christ a similar thing happened to you (Ephesians 1:5)! As His child, you're entitled to a stockpile of spiritual riches.

In Ephesians 1:3, God says He has blessed you with ALL spiritual blessings in Christ Jesus. As a child of God, you're a spiritual tycoon! But what would happen if the richest man in the world adopted you, and you were never told? You would miss out on the joy of being a part of his family. Sadly, many of God's children are missing out on a number of blessings because they've never taken the time to look into all God's spiritual wealth.

Living the Christian life is like opening a treasure chest. The search for true riches ends with Jesus Christ. He is the "X" that marks the spot. The purpose of this booklet is to introduce you to the lavish portfolio of blessings that belong to you as a child of God. Hopefully, this brief introduction will whet your appetite, encourage you to open your Bible, and dig deeper into your own relationship with God.

A DEAD END

Before coming to Christ our problem was simple; we were spiritually dead (Ephesians 2:1). We weren't maladjusted, or immature, or even sick—but dead! God created the first man, Adam, as a three dimensional being with a body, a mind, and a spirit. With his body Adam related to the world around him, with his mind he related to himself, and with his spirit he related to God.

God told Adam that if he sinned he would surely die! Adam bit the forbidden fruit and became poisoned with sin. As God had warned, Adam died, but in a unique way. His lungs continued to inhale and exhale. His heart kept pumping blood. Brainwaves still ricocheted around his cranium, but spiritually he had died. Adam's sin prohibited him from relating to God.

The Bible defines death as separation. According to James 2:26 people die physically when their spirit leaves their body. Likewise people die spiritually when rebellion separates them from God (Isaiah 59:2). Before we came to Christ we were spiritually dead. God intended for the body and mind to act in cooperation with the spirit. We were designed to run on three cylinders, but sin kills the spirit, and limits us to two. God designed us for high performance, but instead we find ourselves sputtering, skipping, and misfiring.

Common sense tells us there are three characteristics of a dead person. First, a corpse is unconscious. You can talk about him to his face without fear of hurting his feelings. He's unresponsive to any physical stimuli around him. Someone spiritually dead is equally unresponsive to God. There's a whole realm of spiritual reality of which he is totally unaware.

Second, a corpse is inactive and boring. It is no fun to spend time with a corpse. People who are spiritually dead often find life to be shallow and stale. They lack the freshness and zest for life that comes from knowing God.

Third, a corpse is decaying. Realize, there are no degrees to death. You're either dead or alive. One corpse is not more dead than another. The same is true spiritually. We are either in Christ or apart from Christ—alive or dead. There's no in-between. Look in the crackhouse, see the demented drug addict, then look in the clubhouse, see the sophisticated socialite. There appears to be an enormous difference, but the distinction is superficial. The only difference is the rate of decay. Without Christ both are as dead as a doornail! The book of Genesis tells us that we have inherited a fallen, sinful nature from Adam. Parents don't have to teach their children to disobey. Sin comes naturally. As a result of Adam's sin, all mankind is born spiritually dead. Our world has become the equivalent of a graveyard populated by spiritual stiffs.

Humans are designed with a God-shaped void at the core of their being. Nothing can fill that void; neither wealth, nor popularity, nor drugs, nor sex, nor sports, nor success. Only God can fill the emptiness in man. We are restless until we find our rest in God. But Satan comes rushing into our lives and tries to fill the spiritual vacuum. He appeals to our mind and body, with ways to improve our image or increase our pleasure. He distracts us from God and lures us into a lifestyle where we seek fulfillment through self-gratification.

Living such a life is like going shopping with a bottomless shopping bag (Haggai 1:6). You can buy items all day long and put them in the bag, only to find the bag empty at the end of the day. You end up with nothing and you go broke in the process. Gone is your integrity, your dignity, and your self respect. All that's left are ugly habits and haunting memories. Sadly, the chains of sin are too light to be felt until they are too strong to be broken.

JESUS TO THE RESCUE

All classic western movies have one scene in common. The pioneers are surrounded by evil villains. The good guys are almost out of ammunition, their leader is wounded, the troops are discouraged, and all hope seems lost. Suddenly a bugle sounds and out of nowhere a battalion of blue-breasted cavalry comes streaking to the rescue. Our situation was just as desperate. We were disabled, discouraged, and depleted. All hope seemed lost until Jesus came riding to the rescue. But why was such a rescue necessary?

TWO WAYS TO GOD

All religions can be divided into two categories. First are those that provide man with a list of rules and rituals by which he can earn God's favor. Kind deeds, self-discipline, religious observance, sacrificial service, and moral character are offered in exchange for

God's blessing. God's acceptance is purchased by a person's performance. Salvation is the result of man reaching up to God. All but one of the world's religions fall into this category. The one exception is Christianity.

The Bible says there is nothing I can do to be good enough to earn God's approval. Isaiah 64:6 declares, "All our righteousnesses are like filthy rags." The salvation Christ offers is not based on man reaching up to God with good deeds, but God reaching down to man in love. God saw mankind drowning in the roaring rapids of death. Jesus dove in to save us. It wasn't our good intentions that coaxed Christ into the icy waters. Romans 5:8 gives us His reason, "But God demonstrates His own love toward us, in that while we were still sinners, Christ died for us." God loves us!

God loves us with a very special unconditional love. Ephesians 2:8-9 states, "For by grace you have been saved through faith, and that not of yourselves; it is the gift of God, not of works, lest anyone should boast." Our salvation had nothing to do with the deeds we have done or the price you could pay! We're saved by grace. Remember this acrostic, grace is "God's Riches At Christ's Expense." God's favor and forgiveness is a free gift. We receive it not by keeping the rules but by trusting in Jesus. If we could save ourselves, God would never have subjected His Son to the horrors of the cross.

A JOB WELL DONE

Since God was His father, Jesus was born without Adam's sin. At His baptism the Father spoke from heaven saying, "This is My beloved Son, in whom I am well pleased" (Matthew 3:17). Jesus was the only perfect man who ever lived. When Jesus died upon the cross it was not for anything He had done, but our sins were thrust upon His sinless shoulders (2 Corinthians 5:21). Christ died as our substitute. He suffered in our place so that we could be forgiven.

On the cross Jesus cried, "My God, My God, why have You forsaken Me?" (Matthew 27:46) At that moment, Jesus experienced separation from the Father so that we could be restored. When my oldest son was two years old we had to admit him to the hospital. Before the nurses inserted the IV they asked my wife and me to leave the room. They knew the ordeal would be painful, and if we were present my son would wonder why we were allowing this to happen to him. My wife was smart enough to walk down the hall out of earshot, but I stayed just outside the door. When they stuck him with the needle he screamed the most blood-curdling yell I've ever heard. When I heard him scream, "I WANT MY DADDY!" I could've clawed through that door. I could've jerked it off the hinges, but I restrained myself because I knew what was best for my son. Imagine God's reaction when Jesus cried for Him. God wanted to come to the rescue, but the Father remained behind the door because Jesus was paying the price for our sins.

Just before He died, Jesus uttered the victorious cry, "It is finished" (John 19:30). All that needed to be done to guarantee our salvation had been accomplished. Our debt of sin was paid in full. Now to receive God's favor and forgiveness all that's necessary is to believe on Christ. Salvation is free, but never think it's cheap. It cost God His only Son. God's pain was our gain.

RECEIVING GRACE GRACEFULLY

An artist was commissioned to paint a portrait of the prodigal son, a man who ran away from God. He walked the streets for days, sizing up his town's drunks and derelicts, searching for just the right wretched model for his painting. Finally, he found him. The artist asked the indigent man to be at his studio the next morning at ten o'clock. When it appeared the man was late the artist was upset. The only person he had seen in the lobby was a well dressed man in a bright new suit.

After some time the well-groomed man approached the receptionist to inform her that he was here to pose for the painting. The artist couldn't believe the transformation. This couldn't be the dirty, dingy, disheveled man he had picked out. The derelict thought since he was posing for a painting he might as well shower, shave, and buy some new clothes.

The man's efforts to clean himself up and make himself worthy only served to disqualify him for the honor of being the artist's subject. Granted, God doesn't mind our cleaning up. As a matter of fact, now that you've become a Christian, God's first order of business is to cleanse you and free you from your sin. But we can't make ourselves worthy of God's favor with a moral shower and shave. Our problem runs deeper. It took the Spirit of God working in us to bring us from death to life. We had to be changed from the inside out, something the Bible calls being "born again" (John 3:1-15).

God wants us to always come to Him just as we are. We must constantly learn to be humble, to be honest about our sin. Growing in Christ means to admit we could never be worthy of His love, that we could never save ourselves, and to surrender all we are to Jesus Christ. Learn to receive God's grace gracefully. It's an insult to attempt to pay for an item that's given as a gift. God has fully paid the price for our relationship with Him. The best way to say thanks is to simply receive, enjoy and utilize God's free gift of salvation.

WHAT DOES IT MEAN TO REALLY KNOW GOD?

There are people who think their good works and church attendance can purchase them a ticket to heaven. But how can walking into a church building once a week do anything to change man's festering sin and lifeless spirit? Visiting a barn doesn't make you a cow, nor does going to church make you a Christian. A person can act like a cow and moo until he's blue in the face, but it won't make that person a cow. Likewise, a person can walk a church aisle, learn some Christian lingo, and even get involved in Christian activities, but it won't make him a Christian.

Going to church does as much to cure a spiritual problem as sitting down in a hospital lobby does to cure a physical problem. It takes more than a visit to the doctor. Eventually a person has to trust the surgeon to operate.

A friend of mine recently underwent a liver transplant. The surgery saved his life. You've also experienced some life-saving surgery. When you came to Christ He performed a divine transplant. He placed His Holy Spirit into your hollow spirit. In Ephesians 2:5, God says He made you alive together with Christ. God united you with Jesus by placing His Holy Spirit in your heart (1 Corinthians 3:17). In God's eyes you became one with Christ. This is what it means to be "in Christ." Christ lives in you and wants to live through you (Colossians 1:27)!

The Christian life is an exchanged life. As Christ lives in me I swap all that I am for all that He is: my guilt for His grace, my pride for His plan, my hurts for His healing, my pain for His peace, my lust for His love, and my fears for His fortitude.

Galatians 2:20 reads, "I have been crucified with Christ; it is no longer I who live, but Christ lives in me; and the life which I now live in the flesh I live by faith in the Son of God, who loved me and gave Himself for me." As Christ died upon the cross, the old you, the person controlled by sin, also died. The proud, obstinate person that used to stare back at you when you looked in the mirror is dead! You're now a new, improved model.

All of us were at one time sinners, alienated from God. Once in a while we slipped up and did something good, but our nature was hostile and rebellious toward God (Ephesians 2:3). That was yesterday. In Christ you've become a saint. Yes, you will occasionally slip up and sin, but you have received a new nature, a nature that loves God and loves others. In 2 Corinthians 5:17 we're told, "If anyone is in Christ, he is a new creation; old things have passed away; behold, all things have become new."

Occasionally, it's a good idea to put some flowers on the grave of that old man. We can look back and learn from our past life, but in doing so we need to remind ourselves that our old self is dead. You're no longer the same person you once were. If you feel tempted to return to your former lifestyle, remember that's no longer you! You're now a child of God—a new person in Christ.

PROOF POSITIVE

We all know you can't keep a good man down. Three days after His crucifixion Jesus Christ rose from the dead. At one time, the religious leaders of His day approached Jesus and requested a sign. They wanted to know if He really was the Son of God. The only sign He would give them was His resurrection.

That Jesus rose from the dead never to die again should be proof positive that He is in a class by Himself! This is what distinguishes Jesus from other "so-called Saviors." We can visit the graves of Buddha, or Mohammed, or Confucius, and see where these men are buried. But visit Jesus' grave and you'll find it empty!

Jesus' power over death proved His victory over sin. In John 14:6, Jesus said, "I am the way, the truth, and the life. No one comes to the Father except through Me." There are no back doors into heaven. Jesus offers a choice between eternal damnation and eternal delight. He is the fork in the middle of the road.

Suppose you and I were arguing over directions to a distant city, although neither of us had ever been there. We are approached by a person who is a native of our destination. You and I have mustered our best guesses, but this person has made the trip! There are many different opinions floating around about how to enter eternal life, but Jesus came from heaven and returned to heaven. He knows the right directions! He alone has the words of eternal life.

Jesus rose from the dead and later ascended into heaven where He received authority over all of God's creation. Philippians 2:9-11 tells us that God has bestowed upon Jesus "The name which is above every name, that at the name of Jesus every knee should bow, of those in heaven, and of those on earth, and of those under the earth, and that every tongue should confess that Jesus Christ is Lord, to the glory of God the Father." All things are under Christ's jurisdiction. He is the King of kings and the Lord of lords. Christ has earned God's favor and now imparts it to all who call upon Him.

Though God freely offers the gift of salvation, it does not become ours until it is received. Jesus died to take away your sin. He rose from the dead to release you from the effects of sin. He ascended into heaven to become Lord of your life. Jesus now calls the shots and works in you to accomplish His purposes. Christ has done all the work. All we need to do to enter into this relationship is to ask His forgiveness, open our lives to Jesus and commit to following Him.

GETTING A GRIP ON GOD'S GRACE

Romans 3:24 declares that we have been "justified freely by His grace through the redemption that is in Christ Jesus." When God justified us He promised to always treat us just as if we had never sinned. That doesn't mean He ignores or glosses over our sin. When we sin we should confess it and maintain a humble attitude, but sin doesn't end our salvation. The price Jesus paid persuades God to treat me as if I haven't sinned even when I do. Sin is not painless. It breaks God's heart and complicates my life. Yet for the person in Christ sin does not change the reality of our relationship with God.

When we were saved we were completely pardoned. Salvation is not parole or probation. God is not waiting for us to sin so He can strip us of our salvation and send us back to the slammer. All our sin has been forgiven—past, present and future. The only thing needed to maintain our salvation is to believe in the work of Christ on our behalf (Colossians 1:23). Since we were saved by faith, we now need to walk by faith. Colossians 2:6 states, "As you therefore have received Christ Jesus the Lord, so walk in Him."

Many Christians set up their own set of do's and don'ts, and they feel adherence to these rules will make them more pleasing to God. This is a mistake. It's been said, "Being good will keep you out of jail, but it won't keep you out of hell."

In Christ you are as pleasing to God as you can possibly be. Colossians 2:10 says, "You are complete in Him [Jesus]." Your performance cannot improve or diminish your standing with God. God's acceptance is based on the work of Christ, not our own merit. What we do for Christ is a way to express our gratitude for what He's done for us. To serve the Lord will bring us great joy, but it cannot add to what Christ has already accomplished.

A FRIEND IN HIGH PLACES

It's been said "It's not what you know, but who you know that counts." Often the most successful people are not necessarily the most equipped or qualified. A wealthy family, an influential friend, or a diploma from a prestigious college can catapult a person to prominence. You might not have access to wealth, clout, or a formal education, but in Christ you know the most important Person in the universe, no less than God Himself.

In Christ we enjoy the same standing with God as Jesus does. In Ephesians 1:6, God says that He has accepted us in the Beloved— Jesus. Jesus has a permanent pass to the throne of God and He has seen to it you can use His pass anytime you want. Hebrews 4:16 tells us we can come boldly to the throne of grace, that we may obtain mercy and find grace to help in time of need.

Go to God. Love Him. Talk to Him. Depend on Him. Take every aspect of your life to God. He wants to help you. He has given you unlimited access to His unlimited resources. He knows what you need even before you ask. In Matthew 7:7 Jesus tells us, "Ask, and it will be given to you; seek, and you will find; knock, and it will be opened to you." Don't be bashful. God wants to meet your needs.

You will quickly learn that God answers prayer in one of four ways: YES, NO, WAIT, or SOME OTHER WAY. When God says "yes" to one of my prayers I get excited! I tell my friends. I stop people on the street and stand up in church to praise God for what He's done for me. It's reason to rejoice. But I should be just as thrilled when God says "no." God is much wiser than I am. My kids sometimes desire things that look good to them but would prove harmful, and as a responsible parent I have to say no. When God says no to me He is only looking out for my best interests.

Perhaps the toughest answer to swallow is "wait." God loves me and wants to answer my prayers, but He does not always work on my timetable. God's delays test my faith, purify my motives, and build my endurance. I need both faith and patience to receive His promises (Hebrews 6:12).

Finally, God may want to answer your request, but He may chose to do it "some other way." I love making suggestions to God as to how He can answer my prayers. But I get frustrated when He doesn't follow my script (which is most of the time). Learn to let God be God. His will is always best. God does His work in His time and in His way.

HEAVEN IS OUT OF THIS WORLD!

In Ephesians 1:10 God says that in the end He will bring everything that is in Christ into His presence. How exciting to know that the Almighty, Holy God of the universe wants us to spend eternity with Him. There He will show us the full extent of the riches of His love toward us (Ephesians 2:7)!

Heaven is going to be "out of this world"! The earth has some scenic spots. Majestic mountains, babbling brooks, and dazzling sunsets are just a few strokes on God's masterpiece. Shortly before Jesus ascended into heaven He told His disciples He was going to prepare a place for them to live forever. Apparently, Jesus has been working on heaven for 1900 years. If He created this world in just six days think of what heaven will be like after 1900 years of construction!

Not only will we spend eternity in God's Kingdom, we will also reign and rule with Christ. When Jesus ascended into heaven God exalted Him. God's Kingdom was given to Jesus as an inheritance. Romans 8:17 says the Christian is a joint-heir with Christ. As a fellow-heir, you share in both Christ's accomplishments and acquisitions. Jesus will reign for all eternity and we will reign with Him!

Don't get discouraged when God allows you to encounter difficulties. Tough times are God's way of training you for your future position. If we took a scale and placed the hard times we experience on earth in one pan and the glories of heaven in the other, it would be obvious that the glories far outweigh the grind. In the end, the eternal lessons learned from our temporary troubles will be well worth the hardship (2 Corinthians 4:17)!

A Nibble of Heaven

It is true that our grandest blessings are reserved in heaven. Our riches are not of this world, but are of God's Kingdom. Yet in Ephesians 1:14 God tells us that He has given us a down payment on our heavenly inheritance. When we believed in Jesus, God placed within us the Holy Spirit. The Holy Spirit is God's down payment, guaranteeing that He will one day bless us with all that heaven holds.

Running, playing, and riding bikes produces a problem for my kids. After an active day of play they have a hard time dealing with hunger pangs until dinner time. To take the edge off their hunger my wife will give them a little pre-dinner nibble. Our experience with the Holy Spirit is designed with the same purpose in mind. Living in a fallen world creates hunger pangs for heaven. The Holy Spirit provides a little nibble of heaven's glory, joy, and peace.

In John 10:10 Jesus said, "I have come that they may have life, and that they may have it more abundantly." Eternal life doesn't begin when we get to heaven, it begins right here on earth. Eternal life is not just longevity of life, it's a quality of life. The Holy Spirit's influence produces a fruitful, satisfying, abundant life.

The Spiritual Power Plug

The Holy Spirit turns on our spiritual sensitivity and makes us aware of the presence, peace, and power of God. Instead of having to wait to get to heaven to know God, we can sense His presence through the Holy Spirit.

During the Great Depression jobs were scarce. When a telegraph office ran an ad for a new operator, it was no surprise that the office was packed with hopeful candidates. Each person was told to take a number and find a seat in the noisy lobby. One man, a late arrival, rose to his feet and entered the boss' office. The crowd was outraged. How dare this man break in front of people who had been waiting for hours!

A few minutes passed and the man reappeared, this time with the boss. He had gotten the job. Unknown to the clamoring crowd, the boss had been behind the door tapping out the following message in Morse Code: "The first person to enter my office will get the job." This man was the only person to hear beyond the lobby noise and discern the boss' message. This world is like a noisy lobby. God is in the office tapping out messages but no one is sensitive enough to hear them. It's the Holy Spirit who opens our ears and helps us to sense God's promptings.

The Holy Spirit not only communicates to us the presence of God, but also His power (Ephesians 1:19-23). Through the power of the Holy Spirit no habit is too entrapping, no enemy too intimidating, no problem too difficult, no hard time too complicated. The Holy Spirit is the conduit through which the healing power of Jesus is routed into our lives.

In John 7:38, Jesus compared the power of the Holy Spirit to white-water rapids. The Holy Spirit provides an active, vibrant, cleansing stream of supernatural energy that bubbles up within us. It cuts through the rocks of stubborn pride, removes the obstacles of doubt and fear, and carves out a channel through which God's blessings flow. Learn to rely on the power of God available to us in Christ! In 2 Timothy 1:7 Paul states, "God has not given us a spirit of fear, but of power and of love and of a sound mind."

THE RIGHTEOUS RUB

What a privilege it is to know God! He alone is able to satisfy our deepest needs. One of the byproducts of knowing God is becoming like Him. The more we're around a person, the more their influence will rub off on us. This is why we should be careful hanging out with people whose ambitions are evil and self-centered. Yet what an incentive to spend time with God! When I get to know Him, His love, His goodness, and His perspective rub off on me (2 Corinthians 3:18)!

Nothing enriches a person's life like an intimate relationship with Christ (Galatians 5:22-23). In Philippians 3:10-14, Paul said the one goal of his life was to know Christ. All other attractions and ambitions had paled in comparison. His one, consuming desire was the knowledge of Jesus Christ. How exciting life can be when we make Paul's goal our goal!

The blessings and privileges that are ours as a child of God are so extravagant that we expect a little "sticker shock." Obviously, forgiveness of sin, a new nature, access to God, the glories of heaven, an inheritance with Christ, spiritual discernment, the presence, peace, and power of God should carry a very expensive price tag. Our tendency is to wonder how we can afford such a lavish list of blessings. Don't worry! As we have seen, our bill has already been paid by Christ! All God asks us in return is to keep His grace from going to waste.

My grandma loved to cook. It was always dinner time at her house. She cooked a meal for all her visitors. To insult my grandma all we had to do was push aside our plates and tell her we weren't hungry. We learned not to eat before our visit just to make sure we could go back for seconds and make grandma happy. God has set us a table of bountiful blessings. What pleases Him most is for us to "pig out" and keep returning to pack our plates. We insult Him when we fill up on material munchies and push aside His treats.

ROYALTY'S RESPONSIBILITY

When you invited Christ into your life you inherited the most prestigious position on earth. You are now a child of God! President or prince would be a demotion. God is King of the universe and you're His kid. Most of us never thought one day we'd be royalty. None of us are worthy of such an exalted calling, but with the Holy Spirit's help it's our responsibility to live out our appointment in a way that will glorify God and bring Him pleasure.

The only President of the United States not elected to the post by the people was Gerald Ford. President Ford inherited the job from Richard Nixon. It was Nixon who kissed the babies, shook the hands, and earned the office. Ford did nothing to gain the position, but from the moment he took office, everyone in the United States expected Ford to be a good president. You did nothing to become God's child. Jesus did all the work for you, and by faith you stepped into office. But now God expects you to live like one of His children!

The Bible briefs us as to the proper protocol for such an exalted position. As we study our Bible, God makes us aware of His perspectives and principles, and how to live life in His name. It's up to us to be quick to apply what we learn. It's encouraging to now that the Holy Spirit will help us. God never calls us to do what He does not equip us to do. God calls us to love one another, but He also pours out His love into our lives. As we spend time in His presence He forges in us His character so His desires become our desires. The Bible provides us direction and encouragement. The Lord works in our lives from the inside out. He alters our actions by transforming our attitudes.

BLESSED TO BE A BLESSING

It may strike you as peculiar that such a high calling demands such a humble attitude. But Ephesians 4:1-2 tells us "Walk worthy of the calling with which you were called, with all lowliness and gentleness, with longsuffering, bearing with one another in love."

Have you ever known a greedy person? They have no confidence in their future or fortune. Their goal is to grab all they can as fast as they can. The irony is they cannot keep it. However, as children of God our tomorrow is certain and our riches are eternal. We're free to care about others because Christ cares so much for us. We can put up with hassles on earth since our perks are in heaven. Christ lives in me and meets my needs, so I can live my life to meet the needs of others. We are heaven's royalty, but on earth we walk humbly. We will one day reign, but today we serve. Our goal is to love others into God's Kingdom!

The best example available of how to walk as God's child is Jesus Himself. Jesus is God. He could've thrown His weight around, used force and intimidation to get His way, but that was not His style. He laid aside the perks and privileges of deity. He declined special treatment. While among us He lived as one of us.

He concerned Himself with others rather than Himself. The King of the universe became a simple servant (Philippians 2:5-10).

A great way to become like Jesus is to study His life. Read the Gospels (Matthew, Mark, Luke, and John) and observe all that Jesus did and said. As you read about His exploits you'll become proud of Him. You'll puff out your chest when you tell someone He's your Savior. You'll realize what an honor it is to follow Him. A desire to be just like Him will swell up within you to walk in His footsteps.

DRESS TO BLESS

I'm not a snazzy dresser. I'm never too concerned with stepping out in style. But I will admit I like dressing appropriately. I would not want to wear a suit to a picnic or a pair of jeans to a funeral. In Ephesians 4:20-24 we're told that as Christians it's important that we dress appropriately, from God's point of view.

In the spiritual sense, how you dress involves how you see yourself. How do you define yourself: a jock? a housewife? a scholar? a musician? a business person? Who you believe yourself to be will effect where you go and what you do. One's identity determines his activities. An athlete trains. A singer sings. A carpenter builds. A chef cooks. And a Christian follows Christ.

Now that you've come to Christ, first and foremost you're a child of God. You need to learn to see yourself as such. Many Christians have never formed an identity in Christ. They live defeated lives simply because they forget who they are and what they have as a child of God. God encourages us in Ephesians 4:23 to "be renewed in the spirit of your mind."

We live in a material and temporal world where a spiritual and eternal perspective is hard to maintain. What happened to Peter often happens to us. Early one morning, just before daybreak, the followers of Jesus were sailing the Sea of Galilee, when suddenly Jesus appeared to them walking on top of the water. Peter wanted to join Jesus in some supernatural surfing. He jumped out of the boat and started walking across the water to meet the Lord, but the waves were rough and the wind was strong. The moment he took his eyes off Jesus and focused on the storm, Peter took a plunge. If we want to succeed in the Christian life we need to keep our attention on Jesus and not get distracted by our surroundings and circumstances.

We get out of a relationship what we put into it. We're saved by faith, but faith is not passive. Faith is an aggressive dependence upon God. To stay focused on Christ we need to read our Bible often and rely on the Holy Spirit's help. Meeting with other Christians, finding avenues for service, and sharing what we know about Jesus with our friends are some practical ways we can express our faith.

Worship is the act of converging all our thoughts on the grandeur and greatness of God. When we worship God we replay in our minds what God has done for us. We concentrate on how much He means to us. As we worship we open our hearts to the Holy Spirit and allow Him to work in our lives. Bible study, fellowship, service, sharing, prayer, and worship all help us identify with Christ.

LIVING IN ENEMY TERRITORY

The Christian life would be a lot easier if we didn't have to live behind enemy lines. The Bible teaches us that a battle currently rages between God and Satan. God's children are often caught up in the middle of this conflict. Any father will tell you if you want to anger him just pick on one of his kids. Satan loves to strike at God by hassling his children. He wants to burglarize the blessings that God has given us.

There are two mistakes we make with Satan. First, we underestimate him. The devil is not a cartoon character, a little imp in red leotards, complete with horns, tail, and pitchfork. Satan's greatest accomplishment is in convincing some people he doesn't exist. Satan is very real. He and his cronies are rabid and ruthless. They are evil beyond imagination. They have no conscience or principle and they are out to get you.

But we shouldn't overestimate him either. Satan is not God's equal. God created him a beautiful angel (Isaiah 14, Ezekiel 28).

Satan chose to rebel against God and he's been rebelling ever since. Satan was defeated by Christ upon the cross (Colossians 2:15)! According to Revelation 20:10 his ultimate destiny is the lake of fire. In the meantime, always remember 1 John 4:4, "He who is in you is greater than he who is in the world."

Satan knows that he is defeated, but as the captain of a sinking ship he wants as many people as possible to drown with him. According to James 4:7, if you take a stand against him he's forced to flee. This is why he resorts to trickery and deception when he attacks. Satan's strategy is to cause you to doubt your identity in Christ. If he can distort how you see yourself he can control what you seek to do. If you don't believe you're a Christian chances are you won't live like one.

In Matthew 4, Satan came to tempt Jesus, and prefaced his appeal by saying, "*If* You are the Son of God." If Satan could've caused Jesus to doubt His identity he would have had Him. Satan will do all he can to cause you to abandon your position in Christ.

DON'T FALL FOR FEELINGS

One way Satan attempts to accomplish his strategy is by getting you to trust in your feelings. Your feelings fluctuate from day to day. One day you're feeling "sky high." The next day a headache brings on the "blahs." Satan tries to convince you to trust in your feelings. He makes you think you must always feel joyful and triumphant to be a Christian. He'll try to convince you that you can't be a child of God if you feel sad or lonely.

Don't allow Satan to trick you! Our salvation is not based on our emotions, but on the truths of God's Word. We should live on facts not feelings. When Satan tempted Jesus, the Lord deflected his attacks by quoting Scripture. Consider this poem: "Three men were walking on a wall, Feeling, Faith, and Fact. When Feeling took an awful fall, then Faith was taken back. So close was Faith to Feeling, that he stumbled and fell too. But Fact remained and pulled Faith back, and Faith brought Feeling too."

The fact is that God keeps His promises. Put your faith in God's unchanging Word not in your own fickle feelings. Our feelings must be treated like an unbroken horse. They have to be saddled and bridled until they are brought under control. They can't be trusted until they're tamed. Trust in facts not feelings.

MORE SATANIC SNARES

Guilt is also a tool of Satan. When you stumble or fall as a Christian, Satan will try to extinguish your faith with guilt. He will make you wonder how you could really be a Christian and commit such a sin. Christians are not sinless. You will slip, but when you do, trust in Jesus. He has already forgiven you. Don't bathe in a tub of self-pity and guilt. Dry off with the towel of faith. Remember, your standing before God has nothing to do with your own performance. You are covered in Christ.

Another weapon in Satan's arsenal is doubt. Many Christians are susceptible to doubt because they feel they need to know all the answers. Satan will hit you with a question beyond your knowledge, and your first inclination will be to panic. But let God's peace overshadow your insecurities. His peace will melt away your doubts with the reality of His presence. It's been said, "The heart has reasons the reason knows nothing about." Let His peace sustain you until you can study your Bible and discover the answer.

Satan often resorts to accusations. He will try to condemn you with sins from your past. He will turn up the volume on your own conscience or use others to hurl stones of accusation. The question is who will you believe, your accusers or Christ? Romans 8:33-34 has a word for us when we're being mistreated or misunderstood; "Who shall bring a charge against God's elect? It is God who justifies. Who is he who condemns? It is Christ who died, and furthermore is also risen, who is even at the right hand of God, who also makes intercession for us." In other words, if God doesn't condemn us what does it matter if others do? Rather than condemning you, Jesus is in your corner. He's pulling and praying for you (Romans 8:31-32).

KEEP THE SUPPLY LINES OPEN

One of Satan's favorite strategies is to alienate you from other Christians. In ancient times when an army besieged a city its first maneuver was to cut off the supply lines. If the city could be isolated from outside support it was only a matter of time before it would weaken and eventually crumble. Satan will do all he can to cut you off from other believers.

Activities that take place on Sunday morning, the urge to sleep late, or a rift with someone at church are all tools Satan will use to keep you from getting together with other believers. It's been said, "If we forsake our fellow Christians, it may easily lead to our forsaking Christ." Without the insight and example of stronger Christians we become prone to discouragement, vulnerable to false doctrine, and lax in our devotion.

Always remember we are stronger together than we are apart. Proverbs 27:17 says, "As iron sharpens iron, so a man sharpens the countenance of his friend." Our secular society tries to throw a fog over good and evil, right and wrong, truth and error. A godless world dulls the edge on our commitment. Getting together with Christian friends tends to resharpen our perspective.

RUN THE RACE

In Hebrews 12 the Christian life is compared to a race. Prior to becoming a Christian you were outside the stadium. As you became more interested in Christianity you made your way to the infield. But when you committed your life to Jesus, you jumped onto the track and became a participant in the race. In the beginning you may not be as graceful or fast or have the stamina of the other runners, but don't get discouraged. You are not running AGAINST them, but WITH them. What's important is you've joined the race!

Understand, the Christian life is a marathon. Many well meaning people have gotten out of the blocks in a hurry only to tucker out before they reached the first turn. Don't be a flash in the pan! Your salvation is just a first step. The Christian life is a lifetime commitment.

For the Christian, the finish line is heaven and the prize is the glory of God. Since so much is at stake we should always be in training. Study the Bible diligently, pray constantly, attend a Bible-believing church regularly, and serve the Lord faithfully. God wants you to enjoy a lifetime of usefulness and an eternity of happiness.

Above all else, trust God exclusively. The Holy Spirit is your coach, your trainer, and your teammate. He promises to always be by your side (Hebrews 13:5-6). Nothing can separate you from His love (Romans 8:38-39). Our greatest troubles will arise when we quit relying on God and take matters into our own hands. It's true, you do have a part to play. So do your best and trust God with the rest!

Philippians 1:6 tells us to be "confident of this very thing, that He who has begun a good work in you will complete it until the day of Jesus Christ." I am a notorious procrastinator. My house is littered with projects I've started and never finished. But what God starts He finishes. He did not save you to have you drop out in the first turn. When you become exhausted, ask Him, and He'll carry you. God won't give up on you, so don't you give up on Him! "Run with endurance the race that is set before us, looking unto Jesus, the author and finisher of our faith" (Hebrews 12:1-2).

"Now to Him who is able to keep you from stumbling, and to present you faultless before the presence of His glory with exceeding joy, to God our Savior, who alone is wise, be glory and majesty, dominion and power, both now and forever. Amen" (Jude 24-25).

THINK IT OVER

A REASON TO REJOICE

1) A parable is a scene from everyday life which illustrates an eternal lesson. In Luke 15 Jesus tells three parables: the lost sheep, the lost coin, and the lost son. The three parables reveal God's perspective on your salvation. Read the chapter and compose a prayer thanking Jesus for what He's done for you.

2) The Bible teaches that God is omniscient, or all-knowing. He knows events before they occur (Isaiah 46:9-10). God knows your weaknesses and already sees your future failures (Psalm 103:13-14), yet He still chose you to be His child. What does this say about God's love for you?

FROM RAGS TO RICHES

1) In Luke 8 Jesus changes a man's life by delivering him from tormenting demons and restores him to health. In verse 39 Jesus tells the man, "Return to your own house, and tell what great things God has done for you." In a few sentences try to express the change Christ has made in your life.

2) Read Ephesians 1-3 and list some of the blessings and privileges that belong to you as a child of God.

A DEAD END

1) Genesis 3:1-8 describes the sin of Adam and Eve. Pay special attention to how the serpent (Satan) tempts Eve. Surprisingly, over the centuries Satan's tactics remain much the same. What lessons do you learn from this passage of Scripture?

2) Read Romans 1:18-32 and chart the downward spiral of a society that ignores God.

ADAM'S REBELLIOUS KIDS

1) Spiritual needs are not met through physical means. Recall a few occasions when you were lonely, rejected, or disappointed. Where did you turn to ease the hurt? How are these needs being met since you gave your life to Christ?

2) Sin damages our lives like an army of locusts ravages a crop. Sin eats away life and vitality. It ruins our usefulness and robs us of our joy. God declares in Joel 2:25–26, "I will restore to you the years that the swarming locust has eaten...You shall eat in plenty and be satisfied, and praise the name of the Lord your God." God promises to restore what sin has spoiled. What does this promise mean to you?

JESUS TO THE RESCUE

1) Religion is a set of rules and rituals. Christianity is not a religion, but a relationship. Jesus brings us into a personal relationship with God who loves us. Catalog a few differences between religion and a relationship with God.

2) In Luke 18:9-14 Jesus tells a parable of two men who went to the Temple to pray. Contrast the differences in their attitudes. What do you suppose were the underlying reasons for these differences?

A JOB WELL DONE

1) Read Matthew 27, Mark 15, Luke 23, and John 19. These chapters record the awful agony of Christ's death upon the cross. As you read try to imagine the pain and torture Christ endured for you. Squeeze the passages of as much meaning as you can and use a grateful heart to soak up His great love.

2) Read the following verses: Micah 7:18-19, Psalm 103:12, Jeremiah 31:34, and 1 John 1:9. What do these verses reveal about God's willingness to forgive us of our sin and the extent of that forgiveness?

Receiving Grace Gracefully

1) In Luke 7:1-10 a sergeant in the Roman army had a servant who became sick. He loved his servant and sent to Jesus for help. The people who approached Jesus on behalf of their friend misrepresented his attitude. How did the centurion's estimation of himself differ from what the elders had portrayed?

2) We live in a performance oriented society. At school, at play, and at work our worth is measured and our status determined by our personal achievements. How does Christianity differ?

A New You

1) "The Christian life is not living my life for God, but God living His life through me." Explain this statement.

2) When an old friend calls to entice you to sin, when a wicked thought etched in your memory floats through your mind, or when an old habit flares up—how should you react?

Proof Positive

1) Read 1 Corinthians 15:1-28. How does the author (the Apostle Paul) validate the resurrection of Jesus? What reasons does he give for its importance?

2) Read Luke 9:23-26, Luke 9:57-62, and Luke 14:25-33. What do you learn about following Jesus?

Getting a Grip on Grace

1) According to Galatians 2:16 how is a person justified before God? If a friend told you, "Hey, I'm a good person. Of course, I'll make it to heaven," how would you respond in light of this Scripture verse?

2) God treats us as if we never sin. How does this assurance bolster and benefit our relationship with God?

A Friend in High Places

1) In Matthew 6:9-13 Jesus gave His disciples a model prayer. We often recite this prayer, but Jesus intended it as a pattern for prayer. He gave us the blueprint, and it's up to us to provide the materials. Study this model prayer and then rewrite it in your own words.

2) In 1 Thessalonians 5:17 we're instructed to "pray without ceasing." Obviously we have to sleep, eat, work, go to school, etc. We can't literally spend twenty-four hours a day in prayer. What do you think this verse means?

Heaven Is Out of This World

1) Read Revelation 21-22 and list some of the characteristics of what life will be like in heaven.

2) Read 2 Corinthians 1:3-4, 2 Corinthians 4:16-18, 2 Corinthians 12:7-10, Hebrews 12:5-11, and James 1:2-4. Give reasons why God would allow one of His kids to undergo hardships and difficulties?

A Nibble of Heaven

1) Twice in Ephesians (1:15-23, 3:14-21) Paul prays for the Christians in Ephesus. In his prayer he describes the ultimate encounter, an experience with the living God. Note the specifics of his prayers and then pray them for yourself.

2) Listed in Galatians 5:22-23 are the by-products, or fruits of the Holy Spirit's activity in our lives. Good fruits are the result of good roots. What does it mean to walk in the Spirit (verse 25)?

THE SPIRITUAL POWER PLUG

1) Read 1 Corinthians 2:9-16. Why do we need the Holy Spirit to understand spiritual truth? Can a person without the Holy Spirit's influence understand the things of God? Why or why not?

2) Before we're saved the Holy Spirit is WITH us drawing us to Christ. When we're saved He comes to dwell IN us (John 14:17). Once we're saved He wants to come UPON us and give us boldness to be a witness for Christ (Acts 1:8). In Acts 4:23-31 the disciples ask God for boldness and He fills them with the Holy Spirit. Study this prayer, pray it for yourself, then be ready for a surge of supernatural strength!

THE RIGHTEOUS RUB

1) All great men of God have one characteristic in common. Read the following verses and note this common characteristic: Exodus 33:18-19 (Moses), Psalm 63:1-8 (David), Jeremiah 9:23-24 (Jeremiah), Philippians 3:10 (Paul).

2) Christians, of all people, need to possess the attitude of gratitude. Psalm 116:12-13 gives three ways we can thank God for His blessings. List them in your own words.

ROYALTY'S RESPONSIBILITY

1) Ephesians 4:25-5:20 describes conduct both proper and improper for a Christian. Take a piece of paper and draw a line down the middle of the page. On the left list inappropriate Christian conduct and on the right list appropriate Christian conduct.

2) Your outlook toward your family is very important to God. Both marriage and parenting parallel spiritual relationships between God and His people. Read Ephesians 5:21-6:4 and 1 Peter 3:1-7. How do you need to change your attitude toward your spouse and kids?

BLESSED TO BE A BLESSING

1) Read 1 John 4:19, 2 Corinthians 5:14-15, and Romans 12:1-2. What should be your motivation for serving God and others?

2) Read Matthew 20:20-28. How does Jesus define true greatness? How does this differ from the world's definition? In John 13:1-17 Jesus washes His disciple's feet. To wash a person's feet was a way of refreshing a weary traveler. Think of a way that you could "wash someone's feet."

DRESS TO BLESS

1) Read Matthew 14:22-33. Imagine you were Peter. What thoughts would have rushed through your mind as you took those first few shaky steps? Would you have been distracted by the waves? Can you name a few of the waves in your life that might divert you from Jesus? When Peter began to sink how did Jesus respond to his cry for help?

2) Study the advice of Paul in Colossians 3:1-4. In the context of this passage define the words "seek" and "set."

LIVING IN ENEMY TERRITORY

1) Study Job 1-2. Satan was brutal in his attacks on Job, but were there limitations on Satan's mischief? Who placed the hedge of protection around Job? What do we learn from this story about satanic attacks on the child of God?

2) Read 2 Peter 5:8. How does Peter describe Satan? What is Satan's desire? How are we to defend ourselves? Describe Paul's warning in Ephesians 4:27. Are you ever guilty of giving the devil an opportunity to tempt you?

Don't Fall for Feelings

1) Recall an instance when a bad mood caused a wrong conclusion. Why aren't feelings a reliable indicator of our standing with God?

2) Consider the great saints of the Bible. Don't think their lives were always joyous and happy. Describe the emotions expressed by Paul in 2 Corinthians 1:8, by Jeremiah in Jeremiah 15:10, and by Job in Job 3:1. Did these men forfeit God's favor just because they experienced moments of despair?

More Satanic Snares

1) Evil thoughts are like birds. You can't stop them from flying over your head, but you can keep them from nesting in your hair. How does 2 Corinthians 10:4-5 instruct us to control our thoughts?

2) In Ephesians 6:10-20 Paul compares the armor of the Roman soldier with the spiritual protection given the Christian. What do you learn from this analogy?

Keep the Supply Lines Open

1) Read Hebrews 10:24-25. What does this passage teach us about our obligations to other Christians?

2) Study 1 Corinthians 12:12-27. What is the "body of Christ"? Are you a member of this body? How is the body of Christ supposed to function?

RUN THE RACE

1) In 1 Corinthians 9:24-27 the Christian life is compared to athletic competition. What do you learn from this analogy?

2) Paul suffered much for the cause of Christ. There were times when he felt like throwing in the towel, but he refused to quit (2 Timothy 4:7)! Paul reveals the reason for his endurance in 2 Timothy 1:12. Read the verse and answer these questions: What did Paul know? Of what was he persuaded? How did this knowledge and persuasion build endurance in his life?